2ND EDITION

GUITAR • VOCAL

TAYLOR SWIFT™

T0039697

ISBN 978-1-70519-263-4

Visit Hal Leonard Online at
www.halleonard.com

World headquarters, contact:
Hal Leonard
7777 West Bluemound Road
Milwaukee, WI 53213
Email: info@halleonard.com

In Europe, contact:
Hal Leonard Europe Limited
1 Red Place
London, W1K 6PL
Email: info@halleonardeurope.com

In Australia, contact:
Hal Leonard Australia Pty. Ltd.
4 Lentara Court
Cheltenham, Victoria, 3192 Australia
Email: info@halleonard.com.au

All Too Well

Words and Music by Taylor Swift and Liz Rose

C5   Gsus4   Am7   Fadd9   Fsus2   F   G   Am

Intro

|C5 |Gsus4 |Am7 |Fadd9 Fsus2 |
|C5 |Gsus4 |Am7 |Fadd9 Fsus2

Verse 1

‖C5 |Gsus4
I walked through the door with you,   the air was cold.
      |Am7 |Fadd9 Fsus2
But something 'bout it felt like home somehow
      |C5 |Gsus4
And I   left my scarf there at your sister's house
      |Am7 |F   ‖
And you've still got it in your drawer even now.

Interlude 1

|C5 |Gsus4 |Am7 |Fadd9 Fsus2 |

Verse 2

‖C5 |Gsus4
Oh, your sweet disposition and my wide-eyed gaze.
      |Am7 |Fadd9 |
We're singing in the car, getting lost upstate.
C5 |Gsus4
Autumn leaves falling down like pieces into place
      |Am7 |Fadd9
And I__ can picture it after all these days.

Pre-Chorus

      ‖C5 |Gsus4
And I know it's long gone and that magic's not here no more.
      |Am7 |Gsus4 |F   G |Am   F
And I might be okay but I'm not   fine at all.   Oh._____

Chorus 1

```
      || C5                        | Gsus4
```
'Cause there we are again on that little town street.
```
   | Am                              | F
```
You almost ran the red 'cause you were looking over at me.
```
         | C5
```
Wind in my hair, I was there,
```
            | Gsus4   | Am7          | Fadd9   Fsus2
```
I remember it all too___ well.

Verse 3

```
      || C5                        | Gsus4
```
Photo album on the counter, your cheeks were turning red.
```
            | Am7                      | Fadd9   Fsus2
```
You used to be a little kid with glassesin a twin-sized bed.
```
      | C5                             | Gsus4
```
And your mother's telling stories 'bout you on the tee-ball team.
```
      | Am7                          | Fadd9   Fsus2
```
You taught me 'bout your past, thinking your future was me.

Pre-Chorus 2

```
   || C5      || C5                       | Gsus4
```
And I know it's long gone and there was nothing else I could do.
```
         | Am                | G            | F   G  | Am Fsus2
```
And I forget about you long enough to forget why I needed to._____

Chorus 2

```
      || C5                   | Gsus4
```
'Cause there we are again in the middle of the night.
```
      | Am7                        | Fadd9     Fsus2
```
We're dancing 'round the kitchen in the refrigerator light
```
            | C5
```
Down the stairs, I was there.
```
            | Gsus4      | Am7         | Fadd9   Fsus2      ||
```
I remember it all too well,   yeah.

Interlude 2

```
      | C5          | Gsus4      | Am7        | Fadd9  Fsus2 | G            |
```

Chorus 3

```
            ‖ C5                          | Gsus4
```
Maybe we got lost in translation, maybe I asked for too much.
```
                    | Am7                        | Fadd9    Fsus2
```
But maybe this thing was a masterpiece till you tore it all up.
```
                | C5
```
Running scared, I was there.
```
                | Gsus4    | Am7        | Fadd9
```
I remember it all too ___well._____

Chorus 4

```
            ‖ C5                          | Gsus4
```
And you call me up again just to break me like a promise.
```
        | Am7                    | Fadd9
```
So casually cruel in the name of being honest.
```
                | C5                      | Gsus4
```
I'm a crumpled up piece of paper lying here
```
            |          | Am7        | Fadd9       ‖
```
'Cause I remember it all,_____all,__ all_____ too well.

Interlude 3

```
    | C5          | Gsus4        | Am7          | Fadd9  Fsus2      ‖
```


Verse 4

```
    C5                          | Gsus4
```
Time won't fly, it's like I'm   paralyzed by it.
```
        | Am7                        | Fadd9
```
I'd like to be my old self again, but I'm still trying to find it.
```
        | C5                          | Gsus4
```
After plaid shirt days and nights when you made me your own.
```
        | Am7                  | Fadd9
```
Now you mail back my things and I walk home alone.

4

Verse 5

```
             || C5                    | Gsus4
But you keep my old scarf from that very first week
               | Am7                      | Fadd9    Fsus2
'Cause it reminds you of innocence and it smells like me.
               | C5
You can't get rid of it
               | Gsus4         | Am7    | Fadd9
'Cause you remember it all too__ well,__ yeah.
```

Chorus 5

```
             || C5                    | Gsus4                |
'Cause there we are again when I loved you so,
    Am7      Am7                       | Fadd9
Back before you lost the one real thing you've ever known.
               | C5
It was rare, I was there.
               | Gsus4   | Am7        | Fadd9  Fsus2
I remember it all too__ well.
               | C5
Wind in my hair, you were there,
               | Gsus4
You remember it all…
               | Am7
Down the stairs, you were there,                    ||
               | Fadd9
You remember it all…
               | C5
It was rare, I was there.
               | Gsus4   | Am7        | Fadd9        ||
I remember it all too__ well.
```

Anti-Hero

Words and Music by Taylor Swift and Jack Antonoff

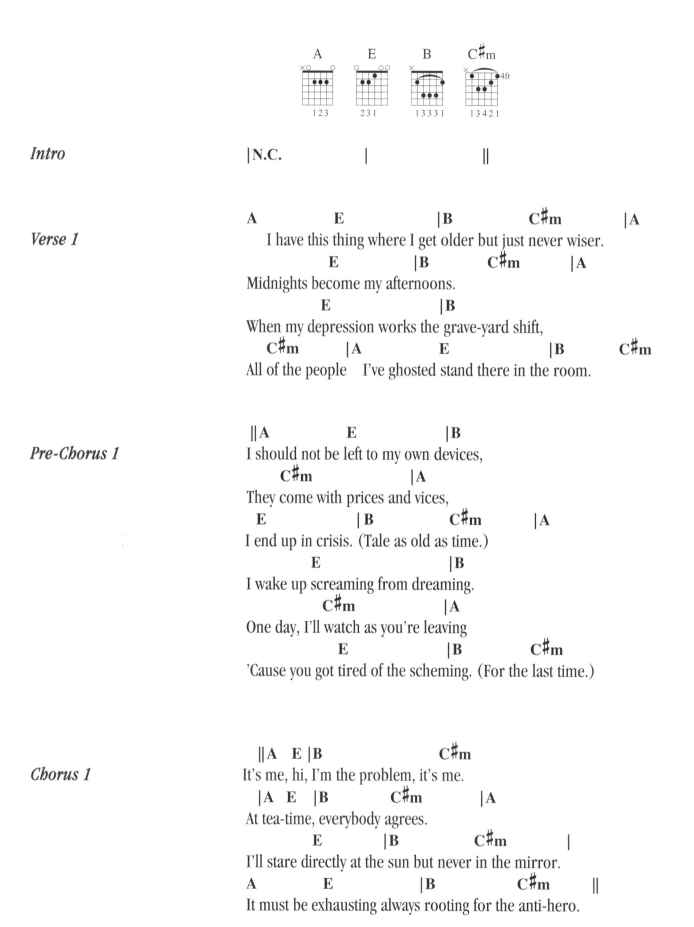

Intro |N.C. | ||

Verse 1

A   E |B   C♯m |A
I have this thing where I get older but just never wiser.
        E |B   C♯m |A
Midnights become my afternoons.
        E |B
When my depression works the grave-yard shift,
  C♯m |A   E |B   C♯m
All of the people   I've ghosted stand there in the room.

Pre-Chorus 1

||A   E |B
I should not be left to my own devices,
  C♯m |A
They come with prices and vices,
  E |B   C♯m |A
I end up in crisis. (Tale as old as time.)
       E |B
I wake up screaming from dreaming.
   C♯m |A
One day, I'll watch as you're leaving
      E |B   C♯m
'Cause you got tired of the scheming. (For the last time.)

Chorus 1

||A E |B   C♯m
It's me, hi, I'm the problem, it's me.
|A E |B   C♯m |A
At tea-time, everybody agrees.
      E |B   C♯m |
I'll stare directly at the sun but never in the mirror.
A   E |B   C♯m ||
It must be exhausting always rooting for the anti-hero.

Interlude 1 |A   E |B   C#m   ‖

Verse 2

A   E |B   C#m |A
    Sometimes I feel like everybody is a sexy baby
        E |B   C#m |A
And I'm a monster on the hill.
        E |B   C#m |A
Too big to hang out, slowly lurching toward your favorite city.
             E |B   C#m   ‖
Pierced through the heart but never killed.

Pre-Chorus 2

A   E |B
    Did you hear my covert narcissism
C#m |A
I disguise as altruism
    E |B   C#m |A
Like some kind of congressman? (Tale as old as time.)
        E |B
I wake up screaming from dreaming.
        C#m |A
One day, I'll watch as you're leaving
        E |B   C#m
And life will lose all its meaning. (For the last time.)

Chorus 2   *Repeat Chorus 1*

Interlude 2   *Repeat Interlude 1*

<pre>
                                    A   E | B   C♯m |A
Verse 2   I have this dream, my daughter-in-law kills me for the money
                                                   E |B   C♯m |A
                            She thinks I left them in the will.
                                                       E |B   C♯m |A
                            The family gathers 'round and reads it and the someone screams out,
                                                    E |B   C♯m
                            "She's laughing up at us from hell!"

                                    ‖A   E |B   C♯m
Chorus 3   It's me, hi, I'm the problem, it's me.
                                     |A   E |B   C♯m
                            It's me, hi,   I'm the problem, it's me.
                                     |A   E |B   C♯m |A   E |B   C♯m
                            It's me, hi,   everybody agrees, everybody agrees.

Chorus 4   Repeat Chorus 1

Outro |A   E |B   N.C.   ‖
</pre>

8

Willow

Words and Music by
Taylor Swift and Aaron Dessner

Em   D   C   G   Am   Bm

Intro

| **Em**   **D** | **Em**   **D** |
| **Em**   **D** | **C**   ‖

Verse 1

Em   **D** | **Em**   **D** |
I'm like the water when your ship rolled in that night.

Em   **D** | **C** | **Em**
Rough on the surface, but you cut through like a knife.

        D | **Em**
And if it was an open-shut case,

       D | **Em**
I never would have known from the look on your face.

    D | **C**   ‖
Lost in your current like a priceless wine.

Chorus 1

G   **D** | **Am**
   The more that you say, the less I know.

      Em | **G**
Wherever you stray, I fol - low.

      D | **Am**
I'm begging for you to take my hand,

    Em | ‖
Wreck my plans: that's my man.

Verse 2

Em   **D** | **Em**   **D** |
Life was a willow and it bent right to your wind.

Em   **D** | **C** | **Em**
Head on the pillow, I could feel you sneaking   in.

      D | **Em**
As if you are a mythical thing,

      D | **Em**
Like you were a trophy or a champion ring.

      D | **C**   ‖
And there was one prize I'd cheat to win.

Chorus 2

G   D |Am
  The more that you say, the less I know.
      Em |G
Wherever you stray, I fol - low.
      D |Am
I'm begging for you to take my hand,
    Em |G
Wreck my plans: that's my man.
      D |Am
You know that my train could take you home;
    Em |G
Anywhere else is hol - low.
      D |Am
I'm begging for you to take my hand,
    Em | ‖
Wreck my plans: that's my man.

Bridge

|Bm   Em |
Am   G |Bm Em |Am
Life was a willow and it bent right to your wind.
        G |Bm Em |
They count me out time and time again.
Am   G |Bm Em |Am
Life was a willow and it bent right to your wind.
     G | N.C. ‖
I come back stronger than a nineties trend.

Verse 3

Em   D |Em D |
Wait for the signal and I'll meet you after dark.
Em   D |C |Em
Show me the places where the others gave you scars.
     D |Em
Now this is an open-shut case,
       D |Em
I guess I should have known from the look on your face.
     D |C
Every bait and switch was a work of art.

Chorus 3

    G   **D**   **|Am**
The more that you say, the less I know.
                Em   **|G**
Wherever you stray, I fol - low.
                D   **|Am**
I'm begging for you to take my hand,
              Em   **|G**
Wreck my plans: that's my man.

                D   **|Am**
You know that my train could take you home;
           Em   **|G**
Anywhere else is hol - low.
                D   **|Am**
I'm begging for you to take my hand,
              Em   **|G**
Wreck my plans: that's my man.

                D   **|Am**
The more that you say, the less I know.
                Em   **|G**
Wherever you stray, I fol - low.
                D   **|Am**
I'm begging for you to take my hand,
              Em   **|G**
Wreck my plans: that's my man.

                D   **|Am**
You know that my train could take you home;
           Em   **|G**
Anywhere else is hol - low.
                D   **|Am**
I'm begging for you to take my hand,
              Em   **|G**   **D**
Wreck my plans: that's my man.
                |Am   **Em**
Hey, that's my man.
                |G   **D**
Yeah, that's my man.
                |Am
Yeah, that's my man.
              Em   **|G**
Every bait and switch was a work of art.
          D **|Am**   **Em**   **|G**
That's my man,   hey, that's my man.
                D   **|Am**
I'm begging for you to take my hand,
              Em   **|**   **N.C.**   **||**
Wreck my plans: that's my man.

Outro   **|Am**   **Em**   **|**

                   ‖: G   **D**   **|Am**   **Em**   **:‖**

Back to December

Words and Music by
Taylor Swift

(Capo 2nd fret)

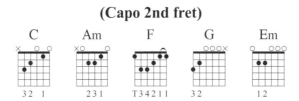

Intro

‖:C |Am   F   :‖

Verse 1

C |Am
I'm so glad you made time to see me.
                                      |F
How's life? Tell me, how is your fam'ly?
               |C   G |C
I haven't seen them in awhile.
                            |Am
You've been good, busier than ever.
                           |F
We small talk, work and the weather.
                        |C   G ‖
Your guard is up and I know why.

Pre-Chorus 1

Am   G
  Because the last time   you saw me
    |C   F
Is still burned in the back of your mind.
    |Am   G |F
You gave me roses and I left them there to die.

Chorus 1

‖C
So this is me swallowin' my pride,

　　　　　　|Em　　　　　　　　　　　　　　　　　|F
Standin' in front of you sayin' I'm sorry for that night.

　　　　|C　　　　　　　　G
And I go back to December all the time.

　　|C　　　　　　　　　　　　　　　　　　　　　　|
It turns out freedom ain't nothin' but missin' you,

Em　　　　　　　　　　　　　　　　|F
Wishin' I'd realized what I had when you were mine.

　　　|C　　　　　　G　　　　　　　　　|F
I go back to December, turn around and make it al - right.

　　　|Am　　　　　　G　　　　‖
I go back to December all the time.

Interlude 1　　　　‖: C　　　　　|Am　　F　:‖

　　　　　　　C　　　　　　　　　　　　　　　　|
Verse 2　　　 These days I haven't been sleepin'.

　　　　　　Am　　　　　　　　　　　　|F
Stayin' up playin' back myself leavin'.

　　　　　　　　　　　　　　　　　　　　|C　　G
When your birthday passed and I didn't call.

　　　|C
And I think about summer, all the beautiful times

|Am
I watched you laughin' from the passenger side

　　|F　　　　　　　　　　　　|C G　　‖
And　 realized I loved you in the fall.

　　　　　　Am　　　　　　　　G
Pre-Chorus 2　 And then the cold came,　 the dark days

　　　　　|C　　　　　　　F
When fear crept into my mind.

　　　　　　　|Am　　　　　　G　　　　　|F
You gave me all your love and all I gave you was　 goodbye.

Chorus 2

‖ C
So this is me swallowin' my pride,

│ Em   │ F
Standin' in front of you sayin' I'm sorry for that night.

│ C   G
And I go back to December all the time.

│ C   │
It turns out freedom ain't nothin' but missin' you,

Em   │ F
Wishin' I'd realized what I had when you were mine.

│ C   G   │ F
I go back to December, turn around and change my own mind.

│ Am   G   ‖
I go back to December all the time.

Interlude 2

‖: C   │ Am   F   :‖

Bridge

‖ Am   F
I miss your tan skin, your sweet smile.

│ C   G
So good to me, so right.

│ Am   F   │ C
And how you held me in your arms that September night,

G   │ Am
The first time you ever saw me cry.

│ F   │ C
Maybe this is wishful thinkin',   probably mindless dreamin',

│ G
But, if we loved again I swear I'd love you right.

│ Am   G   │ F
I'd go back in time and change it, but I can't.

│ Am   G   │ F
So if the chain is on your door, I under - stand.

Chorus 3

‖**C**
But this is me swallowin' my pride,

　　　　|**Em**　　　　　　　　　　　　|**F**
Standin' in front of you sayin' I'm sorry for that night.

　　　　|**C**　　　　**G**
And I go back to December.

　|**C**　　　　　　　　　　　　　　　|
It turns out freedom ain't nothin' but missin' you,

Em　　　　　　　　　　　　|**F**
Wishin' I'd realized what I had when you were mine.

　|**C**　　　　　　**G**　　　　　　　|**F**
I go back to December, turn around and make it al - right.

　|**Am**　　　　　**G**　　　　　　　　|**F**
I go back to December, turn around and change my own mind.

　|**Am**　　　　　**G**　　　|
I go back to December all the time.

Outro　　　　　　|**C**　　　　|**Am**　**F**　　　|**C**　　　|
　　　　　　　　　　　　　　　　　　　All the time.

　　　　　　　　|**Am**　**F**　|　　　　　|　　　‖

Blank Space

Words and Music by
Taylor Swift, Max Martin
and Shellback

(Capo 5th fret)

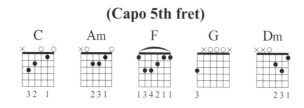

Intro

| N.C.(C) | ‖

Verse 1

C
  Nice to meet you. Where you been?
              |**Am**
I could show you incredible things.

Magic, madness, heaven, sin.
                |**F**
Saw you there and I thought, "Oh, my God. Look at that face."

You look like my next mistake.
G
Loves a game. Wanna play?   Ay.

Verse 2

```
            C                           |
              New money, suit and tie.

                                 |Am
            I can read you like a magazine.

                        |                              |F
            Ain't it funny? Rumors fly and I know you heard about me.

                           |                            |
            So hey, let's be friends. I'm dyin' to see how this one ends.
            G                          |
            Grab your passport and my hand.
            N.C.                                 ‖
            I can make the bad guys good for a weekend.
```

Chorus 1

```
            C                    |                        |Am
             So it's gonna be forever, or it's gonna go down in flames.

                              |                             |Dm
            You can tell me when it's over, mm, if the high was worth the pain.

                        |                    |F
            Got a long list of ex-lovers, they'll tell you I'm insane.

                           |                   |C
            'Cause you know I love the players, and you love the game.

                           |                       |Am
            'Cause we're young and we're reckless. We'll take this way too far.

                        |              |Dm
            It'll leave you breathless, hmm, or with a nasty scar.

                        |                    |F
            Got a long list of ex-lovers, they'll tell you I'm insane.

                        |   N.C.                     ‖
            But I've got a blank space, baby,    and I'll write your name.
```

Interlude | N.C.(C) | ‖

Verse 3

```
C                       |                                    |Am
  Cherry lips, crystal skies. I could show you incredible things.
                        |                                    |F
Stolen kisses, pretty lies. You're the king, baby, I'm your queen.
                              |                          |
Find out what you want, be that girl for a month.
G                       |            |C
Wait, the worst is yet to come. Oh, no!
                        |                              |Am
Screaming, crying, perfect storms. I can make all the tables turn.
                        |
Rose garden filled with thorns.
                        |F                              |
Keep you second-guessin' like, "Oh, my God. Who is she?"
                              |G                    N.C.
I get drunk on jealousy. But you'll come back each time you leave
                  |                                        ‖
```

'Cause darling, I'm a nightmare dressed like a daydream.

Chorus 2   *Repeat Chorus 1*

Bridge

```
N.C.            |                    |
  Boys only want love if it's torture.
                  |                        |
Don't say I didn't, say I didn't warn ya.
                  |                  |
Boys only want love if it's torture.
                  |                  ‖
Don't say I didn't, say I didn't warn ya.
```

Chorus 3   *Repeat Chorus 1*

Cardigan

Words and Music by
Taylor Swift and Aaron Dessner

(Capo 1st fret)

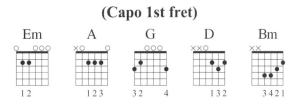

Intro
| N.C.   ‖

Verse 1

    Em | **A**
    Vintage tee, brand-new phone,
          | **G**
High heels on cobblestones.

                 | **A** ‖
When you are young, they assume you know nothing.

Verse 2

    Em | **A**
    Sequin smile, black lipstick,
       | **G**
Sensual politics.

                 | **A** ‖
When you are young, they assume you know nothing.

Chorus 1

D |A

 But I knew you, dancin' in your Levi's,

Drunk under a streetlight.

|G |A

I, I knew you, hand under my sweatshirt,

           |Em

Baby, kiss it better. I…

           |A

And when I felt like I was an old cardigan

        |G

Under someone's bed,

            |A   ‖

You put me on and said I was your fav'rite.

Verse 3

Em |A

 A friend to all is a friend to none.

         |G

Chase two girls, lose the one.

            |A   ‖

When you are young, they assume you know nothing.

Chorus 2

D |A

 But I knew you, playing hide-and-seek

And giving me your weekends.

|G |A

I, I knew you, your heartbeat on the High Line

         |G

Once in twenty lifetimes. I…

           |Bm

And when I felt like I was and old cardigan

        |D

Under someone's bed,

           |G   ‖

You put me on and said I was your fav'rite.

Interlude

|G |Bm |A |G

Bridge

       ‖G |Bm

To kiss in cars and downtown bars was all we needed.

      |A |G   ‖

You drew stars around my scars, but now I'm bleeding.

Chorus 3

      D   **|A**
'Cause I knew you, stepping on the last train,

Marked me like a bloodstain.
|G   **|A**
I,   I knew you, tried to change the ending.

Peter losing Wendy.
|D   **|A**
I,   I knew you, leaving like a father,
                                |G
Running like water. I…
                                            |A
And when you are young, they assume you know nothing.

Chorus 4

                      ‖D
But I knew you'd linger like a tattoo kiss.
             |A
I knew you'd haunt all of my "what ifs."
             |G
The smell of smoke would hang around this long
             |A
'Cause I knew ev'rything when I was young.
             |D
I knew I'd curse you for the longest time,
             |A
Chasing shadows in the grocery line.
             |G
I knew you'd miss me once the thrill expired
             |A
And you'd be standing in my front porch light.
                    |Em
And I knew you'd come back to me.
             |A
You'd come back to me,
             |G
And you'd come back to me,
             |A   **‖**
And you'd come back.

Outro

      G   **|Bm**
And when I felt like I was an old cardigan
                              |D
Under someone's bed,
                                |G   **‖**
You put me on and said I was your fav'rite.

Exile

Words and Music by Taylor Swift,
William Bowery and Justin Vernon

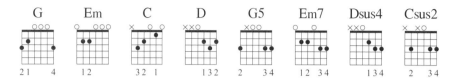

Tune down 1/2 step:
(low to high) E♭-A♭-D♭-G♭-B♭-E♭

Intro |G | Em |G |Em ||

Verse 1 (Male)

            G |Em
   I can see you standing, honey,
                                    |G
With his arms around your body.
                       |Em |G
Laughing, but the joke's not funny at all.
                     |Em
And it took you five whole minutes
                     |G
To pack us up and leave me with it,
                     |Em ||
Holding all this love out here in the hall.

Chorus 1

    C   D |Em
   I think I've seen this film before,
        D |C
And I didn't like the ending.
                  D |Em
You're not my homeland anymore.
        D |C
So, what am I defending now?
                 D |Em   G |C
You were my town, now I'm in exile seeing you out.
             D |Em ||
I think I've seen this film before.

Interlude 1 |G | Em |G |Em ||
        Oo, _____ oo, _____ oo._____

Verse 2 (Female)

G |Em
I can see you staring, honey,

                        |G
Like he's just your understudy,

                         |Em |G
Like you'd get your knuckles bloody for me.

                     | Em
Second, third and hundredth chances,

                  |G
Balancing on breaking branches,

                 |Em ||
Those eyes add insult to injury.

Chorus 2

C   D |Em
I think I've seen this film before,

   D |C
And I didn't like the ending.

       D |Em
I'm not your problem anymore.

 D |C
So who am I offending now?

      D |Em   G |C
You were my crown, now I'm in exile seeing you out.

      D |Em
I think I've seen this film before

         D ||
So I'm leaving out the side door.

Bridge 1 (Male)

```
        G5                |Em7
          So step right out,
                  |Dsus4          |Csus2
There is no amount of crying I can do for you.
          |G5                              |Em7
All this time, we always walked a very thin line.
                          |Dsus4
You didn't even hear me out.
                                (You didn't even hear me…
                                  |Csus2
You never gave me a warning sign.
…out.)                 (I gave so…
          |G5                              |Em7
   All this time, I never learned to read your mind.
…many signs)                         (Never learned to read my…
                  |Dsus4
I couldn't turn things around
…mind.)          (You never turned things…
                                  |Csus2          |G5
   'Cause you never gave a warning sign.
   around.)                      (I gave so may signs.)
          |Em7              |D
So many signs, so many signs.)
                          |Csus2
You didn't even see the signs.
```

Chorus 3 (Both)

```
   C          D              |Em
   I think I've seen this film before,
       D                  |C
And I didn't like the ending.
                 D          |Em
You're not my homeland anymore.
       D              |C
So, what am I defending now?
                 D              |Em          G        |C
You were my town, now I'm in exile seeing you out.
                 D              |Em
I think I've seen this film before.
                          D          ||
So I'm leaving out the side door.
```

Bridge 2 (Male)

G5 |Em7
So step right out,
        |Dsus4 |Csus2
There is no amount of crying I can do for you.
        |G5 |Em7
All this time, we always walked a very thin line.
            |Dsus4
You didn't even hear me out.
                (You didn't even hear me…
              |Csus2
You never gave me a warning sign.
…out.)   *(I gave so…*
        |G5 |Em7
All this time, I never learned to read your mind.
…many signs.)   *Never learned to read my…*
           |Dsus4
I couldn't turn things around
…mind.)   *(You never turned things…*
             |Csus2
'Cause you never gave a warning sign.
around.)   *(I gave so…*
       |G5 |Em7
All this time, I never learned to read your mind.
…many signs.)   *(So many times.)*
           |Dsus4
   I couldn't turn things around
(So many signs.)
              |Csus2 |
'Cause you never gave a warning sign.
            …never gave a warning sign.
                   …never gave a warning…
G5 |Em7
Sign. _____
    |Dsus4 |Csus2   ‖
Ah, _____ ah. _____

Fearless

Words and Music by Taylor Swift,
Liz Rose and Hillary Lindsey

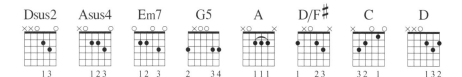

(Capo 3rd fret)

Intro
           |Dsus2 |Asus4 |Em7 |G5 |
   |Dsus2 |Dsus2 |Asus4 |Em7 |G5 ||

           Dsus2 |Asus4
Verse 1   There's something 'bout the way
                   |Em7
       The street looks when it's just rained.
             |G5
       There's a glow off the pavement.
             |Dsus2
       You walk me to the car
               |Asus4
       And you know I wanna ask you to dance
          |Em7 |G5
       Right there in the middle of the parking lot.
          ||
       Yeah.

   |Dsus2 |Dsus2 |Asus4 |Em7 |G5 ||
Interlude 1   Oh, yeah.

Verse 2

    Dsus2   **|Asus4**
      We're driving down the road,
            |Em7
I wonder if you know
           |G5   **|Dsus2**
I'm trying so hard not to get caught up now.
            |

But you're just so cool,
Asus4   **Asus4**   **|Em7**
Run your hands through your hair,
       |G5   **Asus4**   **||**
Absent-mindedly makin' me want you.

Chorus 1

    D5   **|Asus4**   **|Em7**
And I don't know how it gets better than this.
             |G5
You take my hand and drag me head-first.
A   **|D5**
Fearless.

           |
And I don't know why,
Asus4   **Asus4**   **|Em7**   **|G5**
But with you I'd dance in a storm in my best dress.
A   **||**
Fearless.

Interlude 2   **|Dsus2**   **|Asus4**   **|Em7**   **|G5**   **||**

Verse 3

```
Dsus2                    |Asus4
    So, baby, drive slow
                    |Em7              |G5
'Til we run outta road in this one-horse town.
                        |Dsus2              |Asus4
I wanna stay right here in this passenger seat.
                    |Em7
You put your eyes on me.
                    |G5
In this moment now, capture it,
    A          ||
Remember it.
```

Chorus 2

```
Dsus2                |Asus4          |Em7
    'Cause I don't know how it gets better than this.
                        |G5
You take my hand and drag me head-first.
A          |Dsus2
Fearless.

                    |
And I don't know why,
Asus4          |Em7              |G5
But with you I'd dance in a storm in my best dress.
A          ||
Fearless.
```

Guitar Solo

```
|Em7          |G5          |Dsus2          |Asus4          D/F♯|
                    Oh, oh.
|Em7          |G5          |Dsus2          |Asus4          G/B ||
```

Bridge

```
                         C                          |D
             Well, you stood there with me in the doorway.
                 |Em7              D/F♯     |G5    Asus4
             My hands shake, I'm not     usually this way,
                  |C                          |D
             But    you pull me in and I'm a little more brave.
                     |Em7         D/F♯      |G5              |Asus4
             It's a first kiss, it's flawless, really something.
                             ‖
             It's fearless.
```

Interlude 3

```
             |Dsus2        |Asus4      |Em7          |G5              ‖
                                     Oh, _____ yeah.
```

Chorus 3

```
             Dsus2                  |Asus4          |Em7
                'Cause I don't know how it gets better than this.
                                            |G5    N.C.
             You take my hand and drag me head-first.
             A    N.C.  |Dsus2
             Fearless.
                                 |
             And I don't know why,
             Asus4          |Em7                   |G5
             But with you I'd dance in a storm in my best dress.
             A          ‖
             Fearless.
```

Chorus 4   *Repeat Chorus 2*

Outro

```
             |Dsus2        |Asus4       |Em7          |G5              ‖
                     Oh, oh,        oh, aw, yeah.
```

I Knew You Were Trouble

Words and Music by
Taylor Swift, Shellback
and Max Martin

(Capo 6th fret)

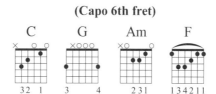

Intro |C | ‖

Verse 1

C | |
Once upon time, a few mistakes ago,

G |
I was in your sights; you got me alone.

|Am |
You found me, you found me,

|F |
You found me - ee - ee - ee - ee.

|C |
I guess you didn't care and I guess I liked that.

|G |
And when I fell hard, you took a step back

|Am |
Without me, without me,

|F | ‖
Without me - ee - ee - ee - ee.

Pre-Chorus 1

C | |G

And he's long _____ gone

| |Am

When he's next _____ to me.

| |F

And I re   -   alize

| ‖

The blame is on me. 'Cause…

Chorus 1

Am |F |G

I knew you were trouble when you walked in,

|C   G |Am

So shame on me now.

|F |G

Flew me to places I'd never been,

|C   G |

Till you put me down, oh.

Am |F |G

I knew you were trouble when you walked in,

|C   G |Am

So shame on me now.

|F |G

Flew me to places I'd never been.

|C   N.C. |Am

Now I'm lying on the cold, hard ground.

|F |G |C   G |Am

Oh, oh, trouble, trouble, trouble.

|F |G |C   G   ‖

Oh, oh, trouble, trouble, trouble.

Verse 2

```
  C                        |
No apologies. He'll never see you cry;
    |G                     |
Pretends he doesn't know that he's the reason why.
       |Am            |
You're drowning, you're drowning,
       |F            |
You're drowning - ing - ing - ing - ing.
      |C                    |
And I heard you moved on from whispers on the street.
   |G                  |
A new notch in your belt is all I'll ever be.
      |Am        |           |
And now I see, now I see,
 F              |              ‖
Now I see - ee - ee - ee - ee.
```

Pre-Chorus 2

```
C            |       |G
 He was long _____ gone
             |       |Am
When he met _____ me.
       |                 |F
And I re       -      alize
             |          ‖
The joke is on me, hey.
```

Chorus 2

Am |F |G
I knew you were trouble when you walked in,

  |C   G |Am
So shame on me now.

      |F |G
Flew me to places I'd never been,

    |C   G |
Till you put me down, oh.

Am |F |G
I knew you were trouble when you walked in,

  |C   G |Am
So shame on me now.

      |F |G
Flew me to places I'd never been.

    |C   G |Am
Now I'm lying on the cold, hard ground.

   |F |G |C   G |Am
Oh, oh,   trouble, trouble, trouble.

   |F |G |C   G   ‖
Oh, oh,   trouble, trouble, trouble.

Bridge

     ‖F | |Am |
And the saddest fear   comes creeping in:

    |F |
That you never loved me,   or her,

 |G | | ‖
Or anyone, or anything,   yeah.

Chorus 3   *Repeat Chorus 2*

Outro

Am |F |G
I knew you were trouble when you walked in.

   |C   G |
Trouble, trouble, trouble.

Am |F |G
I knew you were trouble when you walked in.

   |C   N.C.   ‖
Trouble, trouble, trouble.

Look What You Made Me Do

Words and Music by Taylor Swift, Jack Antonoff,
Richard Fairbrass, Fred Fairbrass and Rob Manzoli

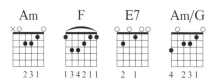

Intro   ‖: **Am** | |**F** |**E7**   :‖

Verse 1

Am | |
I don't like your little games,

     | |
Don't like your tilted stage.

     | |
The role you made me play of the fool.

     | ‖
No, I don't like you.

Verse 2

Am | |
I don't like your perfect crime,

     | |
How you laugh when you lie.

     | |
You said the gun was mine. Isn't cool.

     | ‖
No, I don't like you.

Pre-Chorus 1

     Am | |**Am7**
But I got smarter, I got harder in the nick of time.

                  | |**F**
Honey, I rose up from the dead, I do it all time.

                  | |**E7**
I've got a list of names and yours is in red, underlined.

           | ‖
I check it once, then I check it twice, *oh!*

Chorus 1

     N.C. | |
Ooh, look what you made me do, look what you made me do.

                | |
Look what you just made me do, look what you just made me…

                | |
Ooh, look at what you made me do, look what you made me do,

                | ‖
Look what you just made me do, look what you just made me

Verse 3

     Am | |
I don't like your kingdom keys,
Do.

     | |
They once belonged to me.

     | |
You asked me for a place to sleep,

         | ‖
Locked me out and threw a feast.

Interlude 1

     N.C. | |
The world moves on, another day, another drama, drama.

                | |
But not for me, not for me, all I think about is karma.

                | |
And then the world moves on, but one thing's for sure:

                | ‖
Maybe I got mine, but you'll all get yours.

Pre-Chorus 1   *Repeat Pre-Chorus 1*

Chorus 2   *Repeat Chorus 1*

Bridge

    Am | |**F**
I don't trust nobody and nobody trusts me.
Do.

      |**E7** |
I'll be the actress starring in your bad dreams.

     Am | |**F**
‖: I don't trust nobody and nobody trusts me.

      |**E7**
I'll be the actress starring in your bad dreams. :‖ ***Play 3 times***

Interlude 2

|**Am** | |**Am/G**

      |
"I'm sorry, the old Taylor

     |**F** |
Can't come to the phone right now.

    |**E7** |**N.C.** ‖
Why?   *Oh,*   *'cause she's dead!"*

Chorus 3

    Repeat Chorus 1

Outro-Chorus

Am | |**Am/G**
Do. Look what you made me do, look what you made me do.

             | |
Look at what you just made me do, what you just made me…
F | |**E7**
Ooh, look at what you made me do, look what you made me do.

         |**N.C.** | ‖
Look at what you just made me do, look what you just made me do.

36

Our Song

Words and Music by Taylor Swift

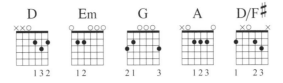

Intro

```
|D          Em        |G        A          |
|D          Em        |G        A
```

Verse 1

```
          ||D                      Em
I was riding shotgun with my hair undone
       |G            A
In the front seat of his car.
            |D                Em
He's got a one-hand feel on the steering wheel,
      |G        A            |D
The other on my    heart.
                    Em
I look around, turn the radio down.
          |G                   A
He says, "Baby, is something wrong?"
    |D            Em           |G              |A
I say, "Nothing. I was just thinking how we don't have a song."
```

Chorus 1

```
          N.C.      ||D            Em                      |
And he says,    "Our song is the slamming screen door,
G                      A              |D
Sneakin' out late, tapping on your window.
                      Em             |G
When we're on the phone and you talk real slow
                        A        |D
'Cause it's late and your mama don't know.
                    Em
Our song is the way you laugh,
     |G                 A                        |G
The first date, 'Man, I didn't kiss her and I should have.'
             |A             |Em
And when I got home, 'fore I said A-men,
          D/F#   G|  N.C.              ||
Asking God__ if He_   could play it again."
```

Interlude 1 |D   Em |G   A ||

                          D   Em
Verse 2   I was walking up the front porch steps
                            |G   A
                          After everything that day
                            |D   Em
                          Had gone all wrong and been trampled on
                              |G   A |
                          And, uh, lost and thrown a - way.
                          D   Em |G   A
                          Got to the hallway, well on my way to my lovin' bed.
                           |D   Em |G   A ||
                          I almost didn't notice all the roses and the note that   said…

                          D   Em |
Chorus 2   "Our song is the slamming screen door,
                          G   A |D
                          Sneakin' out late, tapping on your window.
                                                  Em |G
                          When we're on the phone and you talk real slow
                                                    A |D
                          'Cause it's late and your mama don't know.
                                        Em
                          Our song is the way you laugh,
                            |G   A |G
                          The first date, 'Man, I didn't kiss her and I should have.'
                                    |A |Em
                          And when I got home, 'fore I said A-men,
                                    D/F♯   G | A ||
                          Asking God__ if He__   could play it again."

                          |D   Em |G   A |
Fiddle/Guitar Solo   Da, da, da, da.
                          |D   Em |G |A

Bridge

```
   ||Em                        |G
I've heard every album, listened to the radio,
   |D          A            |Em
Waited for something to come along
                    |G                    ||
That was as good as our song.
```

Chorus 3

```
D                          Em                     |
 'Cause our song is the slamming screen door,
G                     A           |D
Sneakin' out late, tapping on his, uh, window.
                              Em              |G     N.C.
When we're on the phone and he talks real slow
              A            |D
'Cause it's late and his mama don't know.
                  Em
Our song is the way he laughs,
   |G                  A                        |G
The first date, "Man, I didn't kiss him and I should have."
              |A              |Em
And when I got home, 'fore I said A-men,
         D/F♯  G|        A          ||
Asking God__ if He_  could play it again."__
```

Interlude 2

```
   |D        Em        |G       A        |D       Em              |
_____        Yeah.        Uh, play it again_____
|G        A        |D        Em       |G       A
_____    Oh, yeah.____         Huh, oh yeah.
```

Outro

```
        ||D                     Em
I was riding shotgun with my hair undone
    |G          A             |D
In the front seat of his car.
                         Em            |G
I grabbed a pen and an old napkin and I
                       ||
Wrote down our song.
```

Love Story

Words and Music by
Taylor Swift

(Capo 2nd fret)

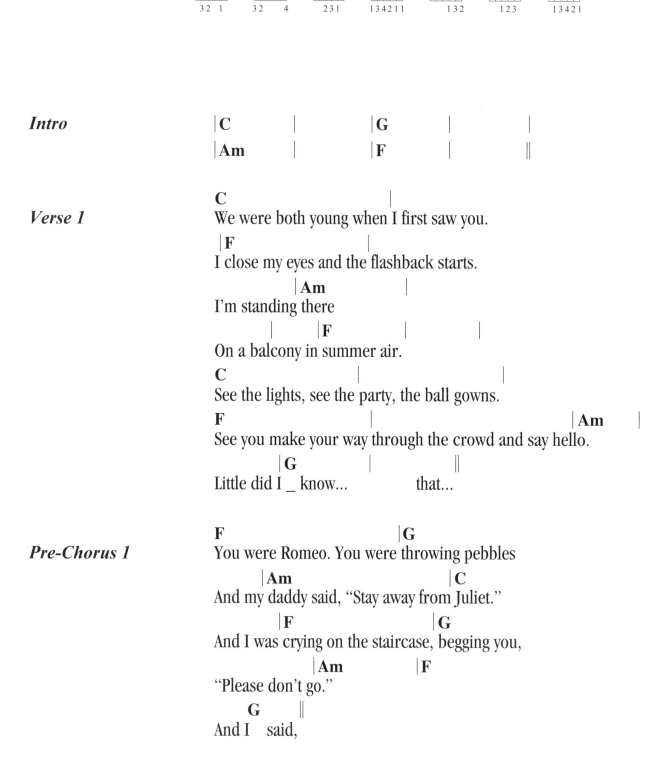

Intro

|C | |G | | |
|Am | |F | | ||

Verse 1

C |
We were both young when I first saw you.
|F |
I close my eyes and the flashback starts.
|Am |
I'm standing there
| |F | |
On a balcony in summer air.
C | |
See the lights, see the party, the ball gowns.
F | |Am |
See you make your way through the crowd and say hello.
|G | ||
Little did I _ know...   that...

Pre-Chorus 1

F |G
You were Romeo. You were throwing pebbles
|Am |C
And my daddy said, "Stay away from Juliet."
|F |G
And I was crying on the staircase, begging you,
|Am |F
"Please don't go."
G ||
And I   said,

Chorus 1

```
C                    |                                        |
"Romeo, take me somewhere where we can be alone.
G                    |                           |
I'll be waiting; all there's left to do is run.
Am                   |                           |
You'll be the prince and I'll be the princess.
F           |G          N.C. |C          |
It's a love story. Baby, just say    yes."
```

Verse 2

```
   ‖C                 |                      |
So I sneak out to the garden to see you.
F                    |
We keep quiet 'cause we're dead if they knew.
              |Am          |
So close your eyes,
                |G          |
Escape this town for a little while.
              ‖
Oh, oh, 'cause
```

Pre-Chorus 2

```
F                       |G
You were Romeo, I was a scarlet letter
     |Am                  |C
And my daddy said, "Stay away from Juliet."
          |F
But you were ev'rything to me,
    |G                  |Am      |F
I was beggin' you, "Please don't go."
      G         ‖
And I _ said,
```

Chorus 2

C | |
"Romeo, take me somewhere where we can be alone.

G | |
I'll be waiting; all there's left to do is run.

Am | |
You'll be the prince and I'll be the princess.

F |G |
It's a love story. Baby, just say yes.

C | |G
Romeo save me. They're try'n' to tell me how to feel.

                         | |
This love is difficult, but it's, uh, real.

Am | |
Don't be afraid, we'll make it out of this mess.

F |G   ‖
It's a love story. Baby, just say yes."

Guitar Solo

|C | |G | |
                  Oh, oh.

|Am | |F |G

Bridge

            ‖Am |F
I got tired of waiting,

      |C |G
Wondering if you were ever coming around.

        |Am |F
My faith in you was   fading

      |C |G   ‖
When I met you on the outskirts of town and I said,

Chorus 3

```
C                      |                           |
"Romeo save me. I've been feeling so alone.
G            |
I keep waiting for you, but you never come."
 |Am                   |
Is this in my head? I don't know what to think.
 |F                 |G              N.C.      ‖
He knelt to the ground and pulled out a ring and said,
```

Chorus 4

```
D                      |                           |
"Marry me, Juliet. You'll never have to be alone.
A            |
I love you and that's all I really know.
|Bm                    |                           |
I talked to your dad, go pick out a white dress.
G          |A           |D        |
It's a love story. Baby, just say   yes."
        |A           |
Oh, oh. ___
            |Bm        |
Oh, oh, oh. ___
        |G                      |          |D      ‖
'Cause we were both young when I first saw you.
```

Mean

Words and Music by
Taylor Swift

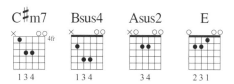

Verse 1

C#m7 |**Bsus4** |**Asus2**
You, with your words like knives and swords
| |
And weapons that you use against me,
C#m7 |**Bsus4** |**Asus2**
You have knocked me off my feet again,
| |
Got me feeling like a nothing.
C#m7 |**Bsus4** |**Asus2**
You, with your voice like nails on a chalkboard,
| |
Calling me out when I'm wounded.
C#m7 |**Bsus4** |**Asus2** | ||
You,   picking on the weaker man.

Pre-Chorus 1

Bsus4 |**E**
   Well, you can take me down
|**Asus2** |**Bsus4** |
With just one single blow.
|**Asus2** | ||
But you don't know what you don't know.

Chorus 1

E |Bsus4 |C♯m7 |Asus2
Someday, I'll be   living in a big ol' city,
    |E |Bsus4 |Asus2 |
And all you're ever gonna be is mean.
E |Bsus4 |C♯m7 |Asus2
Someday, I'll be   big enough so you can't hit me,
    |E |Bsus4 |Asus2 |
And all you're ever gonna be is mean.
   N.C. |E | | | ||
Why you gotta be so ____ mean?

Verse 2

C♯m7 |Bsus4
You, with your switching sides
    |Asus2 | |
And your wildfire lies and your humiliation,
C♯m7 |Bsus4 |Asus2
You have pointed out my flaws again
   | N.C. |C♯m7
As if I don't already see them.
        |Bsus4
I walk with my head down
    |Asus2 | |
Tryin' to block you out 'cause I'll never impress you.
C♯m7 |Bsus4 |Asus2 | ||
I   just wanna feel okay again.

Pre-Chorus 2

Bsus4 | |**E**
    I bet you got pushed around,

       |**Asus2** |**Bsus4**
Somebody made you cold.

          |
But the cycle ends right now,

     |**Asus2** |
'Cause you can't lead me down that road

    | | **N.C.**   ‖
And you don't know what you don't know.

Chorus 2

E |**Bsus4** |**C♯m7** |**Asus2**
Someday, I'll be   living in a big ol' city,

    |**E** |**Bsus4** |**Asus2** | |
And all you're ever gonna be is mean.

E |**Bsus4** |**C♯m7** |**Asus2**
Someday, I'll be   big enough so you can't hit me,

    |**E** |**Bsus4** |**Asus2** |
And all you're ever gonna be is mean.

             |**E** | | | **Bsus4** ‖
Why you gotta be so ___ mean?

Mandolin Solo

   |**Asus2**   **Bsus4** |**Asus2** |

Bridge

        ‖**Bsus4** | |**E**
And I can see you years from now in a bar,

       |**Asus2** |**Bsus4**
Talking over a football game,

          | |**E** |**Asus2** |**Bsus4**
With that same big loud opinion but   nobody's listening.

       | |**C♯m7** |**Bsus4** |**Asus2** |
Washed up and ranting about the same old bitter   things.

Bsus4 | |**C♯m7** **Bsus4** |**Asus2** |
Drunk and grumblin' on about how I   can't   sing.

Interlude

                   ‖**E** |**Bsus4** |**C♯m7** |

But all you are is ___ mean.

Asus2 |**E** |**Bsus4**

All you are is mean and a liar

    |**C♯m7** |**Asus2**

And pathetic and alone in life

   |**E** |**Bsus4** |**C♯m7** |**Asus2**

And mean, and mean, and mean, and mean.

Chorus 3

    ‖**N.C.** | | |

But someday, I'll be living in a big ol' city,

     | | | |

And all you're ever gonna be is mean. Yeah!

E |**Bsus4** |**C♯m7** |**Asus2**

Someday, I'll be   big enough so you can't hit me,

   |**E** |**Bsus4** |**Asus2** | | ‖

And all you're ever gonna be is mean. (Why you gotta be so mean?)

Chorus 4

E |**Bsus4** |**C♯m7** |**Asus2**

Someday, I'll be   living in a big ol' city,

  |**E** |**Bsus4** |**Asus2** | |

And all you're ever gonna be is mean.

E |**Bsus4** |**C♯m7** |**Asus2**

Someday, I'll be   big enough so you can't hit me,

  |**E** |**Bsus4** |**Asus2** |

And all you're ever gonna be is mean.

               |**E**   ‖

Why you gotta be so ___ mean?

Shake It Off

Words and Music by
Taylor Swift, Max Martin
and Shellback

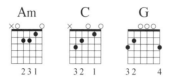

Intro |N.C. | | |

Verse 1

‖**Am** |
I stay out too late,

|**C** |
Got nothin' in my brain;

|**G N.C.** |
That's what people say, mm, mm.

|**G N.C.** |
That's what people say, mm, mm.

|**Am** |
I go on too many dates, ha, ha,

|**C** |
But I can't make 'em stay;

|**G N.C.** |
At least that's what people say, mm, mm.

| |
That's what people say mm, mm.

Pre-Chorus 1

‖**Am** | |**C**
But I keep cruisin'. Can't stop, won't stop movin'.

| **G N.C.**| |**G N.C.** |
It's like I got this music   in my mind sayin', "It's gonna be alright."

Chorus 1

‖**Am** |
’Cause the players gonna play, play, play, play, play,

|**C** |
And the haters gonna hate, hate, hate, hate, hate.

|**G** |
Baby, I'm just gonna shake, shake, shake, shake, shake.

| |
A, shake it off, a, shake it off. (Hoo, hoo, hoo.)

|**Am** |
Heartbreakers gonna break, break, break, break, break,

|**C** |
And the fakers gonna fake, fake, fake, fake, fake.

|**G** |
Baby, I'm just gonna shake, shake, shake, shake, shake.

| |
A, shake it off, a, shake it off. (Hoo, hoo, hoo.)

Verse 2

‖**Am** |
I'll never miss a beat, ah;

|**C** |
I'm lightnin' on my feet.

|**G** **N.C.**|
And that's what they don't see, mm, mm.

|**G** **N.C.**|
That's what they don't see, mm, mm.

|**Am** |
I'm dancin' on my own; (Dancin' on my own.)

|**C** |
I'll make the moves up as I go. (Moves up as I go.)

|**G** **N.C.**|
And that's what they don't know, mm, mm.

|**G** **N.C.**|
That's what they don't know, mm, mm.

Pre-Chorus 2

‖**Am** | |**C**
But I keep cruisin'. Can't stop, won't stop groovin'.

| |**G** **N.C.**| |**G** **N.C.** |
It's like I got this music   in my mind sayin', "It's gonna be alright."

Chorus 2   *Repeat Chorus 1*

49

Bridge

    Am |

Shake it off, a, shake it off.

    |**C** |

I, I, a, shake it off, a, shake it off.

    |**G** |

I, I, a, shake it off, a, shake it off.

    | | ‖

I, I, a, shake it off, a, shake it off, (Hoo, hoo, hoo.)

Breakdown

    N.C. |

Hey, hey, hey.

    |

Just think: while you been gettin' down and out

    | |

About the liars and the dirty, dirty cheats of the world,

    | | | |

You coulda been gettin' down to this sic beat.

    | |

My ex-man brought his new girlfriend. She's like, "Oh my God!"

    | |

But, I'm just gonna shake until the fellow over there

    | |

With the hella-good hair… Won't you come on over, baby?

    | | ‖

We can shake, shake, shake.

Chorus 3

Repeat Chorus 1

Outro

‖:**Am** |

 Shake it off, a, shake it off.

    |**C** |

I, I, a, shake it off, a, shake it off.

    |**G** |

I, I, a, shake it off, a, shake it off.

    | | :‖

I, I, a, shake it off, a, shake it off. (Hoo, hoo, hoo.)

Am |

Shake it off, a, shake it off.

    |**C** |

I, I, a, shake it off, a, shake it off.

    |**G** |

I, I, a, shake it off, a, shake it off.

    | | |**N.C.** ‖

I, I, a, shake it off, a, shake it off.

Sweet Nothing

Words and Music by Taylor Swift
and William Bowery

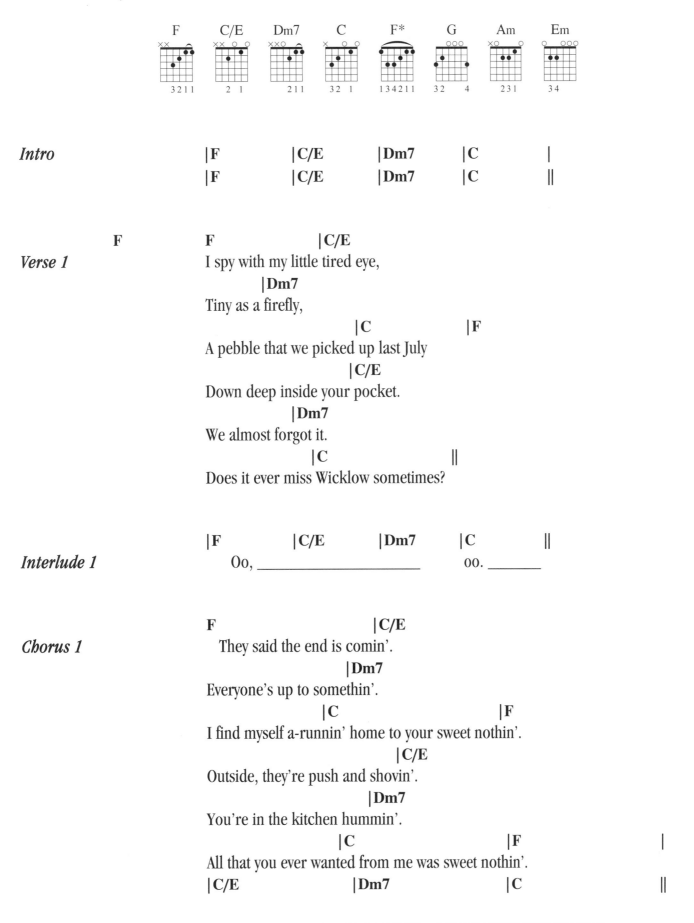

Intro

|F |C/E |Dm7 |C |
|F |C/E |Dm7 |C ||

Verse 1

              F   F |C/E

I spy with my little tired eye,

                 |Dm7

Tiny as a firefly,

                      |C |F

A pebble that we picked up last July

                |C/E

Down deep inside your pocket.

            |Dm7

We almost forgot it.

               |C ||

Does it ever miss Wicklow sometimes?

Interlude 1

|F |C/E |Dm7 |C ||

Oo, _____   oo. _____

Chorus 1

        F |C/E

  They said the end is comin'.

                  |Dm7

Everyone's up to somethin'.

               |C |F

I find myself a-runnin' home to your sweet nothin'.

                      |C/E

Outside, they're push and shovin'.

                 |Dm7

You're in the kitchen hummin'.

               |C |F |

All that you ever wanted from me was sweet nothin'.

|C/E |Dm7 |C ||

Bridge

```
             F                    |C/E
                On the way home
                               |Dm7
             I wrote a poem.
                                 |C
             You say, "What a mind!"
                                 ||
             This happens all the time.
```

Interlude 2

```
             |F              |C/E         |Dm7        |C           ||
               Oo, _____        oo. _____
```

Chorus 2

```
             F                                |C/E
                'Cause they said the end is comin'.
                                  |Dm7
             Everyone's up to somethin'.
                             |C                          |F
             I find myself a-runnin' home to your sweet nothin's.
                                      |C/E
             Outside, they're push and shovin'.
                                      |Dm7
             You're in the kitchen hummin'.
                                   |C                      ||
             All that you ever wanted from me was nothin'.
```

Verse 2

```
             F
             Industry disrupters
                  |C/E
             And soul deconstructors
                  |Dm7                      |C
             And smooth-talking hucksters out glad-handing each other.
                     |F
             And the voices that implore,
                   | C/E
             "You should be doing more."
                |Dm7                |C                    |F                         |
             To you, I can admit that I'm just too soft for all of it.
             |C/E                 |Dm7                         |C                        ||
```

Interlude 3

```
|F          |C/E       |Dm7      |C          ||
   Oo, _____
```

Chorus 3

```
F*                        |G
  They said the end is comin'.
                     |C
Everyone's up to somethin'.
                |Am                      |F*
I find myself a-runnin' home to your sweet nothin's.
                      |G
Outside, they're push and shovin'.
                  |C
You're in the kitchen hummin'.
                   |Em                    |F*
All that you ever wanted from me was sweet nothin'.
                  |G
They said the end is comin'.
                |C
Everyone's up to somethin'.
          |Am                      |F*
I find myself a-runnin' home to your sweet nothin's.
                    |G
Outside, they're push and shovin'.
                |C
You're in the kitchen hummin'.
           |Am                    |F
All that you ever wanted from me was sweet nothin'.
|C/E            |Dm7              |C                    ||
```

Teardrops on My Guitar

Words and Music by
Taylor Swift and Liz Rose

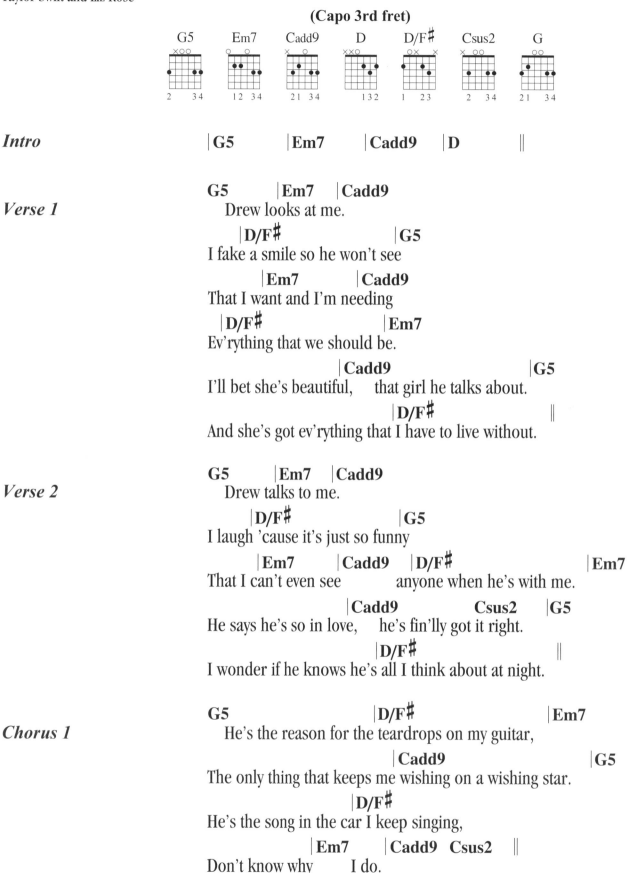

(Capo 3rd fret)

G5   Em7   Cadd9   D   D/F♯   Csus2   G

Intro |G5 |Em7 |Cadd9 |D ||

Verse 1

G5 |Em7 |Cadd9
  Drew looks at me.
     |D/F♯ |G5
I fake a smile so he won't see
        |Em7 |Cadd9
That I want and I'm needing
    |D/F♯ |Em7
Ev'rything that we should be.
                    |Cadd9 |G5
I'll bet she's beautiful,   that girl he talks about.
                         |D/F♯ ||
And she's got ev'rything that I have to live without.

Verse 2

G5 |Em7 |Cadd9
  Drew talks to me.
     |D/F♯ |G5
I laugh 'cause it's just so funny
     |Em7 |Cadd9 |D/F♯ |Em7
That I can't even see   anyone when he's with me.
                    |Cadd9   Csus2 |G5
He says he's so in love,   he's fin'lly got it right.
                    |D/F♯ ||
I wonder if he knows he's all I think about at night.

Chorus 1

G5 |D/F♯ |Em7
  He's the reason for the teardrops on my guitar,
                         |Cadd9 |G5
The only thing that keeps me wishing on a wishing star.
                    |D/F♯
He's the song in the car I keep singing,
               |Em7 |Cadd9 Csus2 ||
Don't know why   I do.

Verse 3

```
G5          |Em7    |Cadd9
   Drew walks by me.
   |D/F♯                    |G5
Can he tell that I can't breathe?
              |Em7        |Cadd9
And there he goes so perfectly,
         |D/F♯                  |Em7
The kind of flawless I wish I could be.
                  |Cadd9        Csus2   |G5
She better hold him tight,    give him all her love,
              |D/F♯                           ‖
Look in those beautiful eyes and know she's lucky 'cause...
```

Chorus 2

Repeat Chorus 1

Guitar Solo

```
|G5        |Em7      |Cadd9      |D/F♯       ‖
```

Pre-Chorus

```
Em7                 |Cadd9                    |G5
So I drive home alone.    As I turn out the light,
                  |D/F♯                       ‖
I'll put his picture down and maybe get some sleep tonight.
```

Chorus 3

```
G5                          |D/F♯                |Em7
   'Cause he's the reason for the teardrops on my guitar,
                  |Cadd9                      |G5
The only one who's got enough of me to break my heart.
              |D/F♯                         |Em7     |Cadd9
He's the song in the car    I keep singing, don't know why I do.
Csus2  |G5                    |D/F♯
He's the time taken up, but there's never enough
          |Em7          |Cadd9   Csus2   ‖
And he's all that I need to fall into.
```

Outro

```
G5      |Em7   |Cadd9
Drew looks at me,
   |D/F♯               |G         ‖
I fake a smile so he won't see.
```

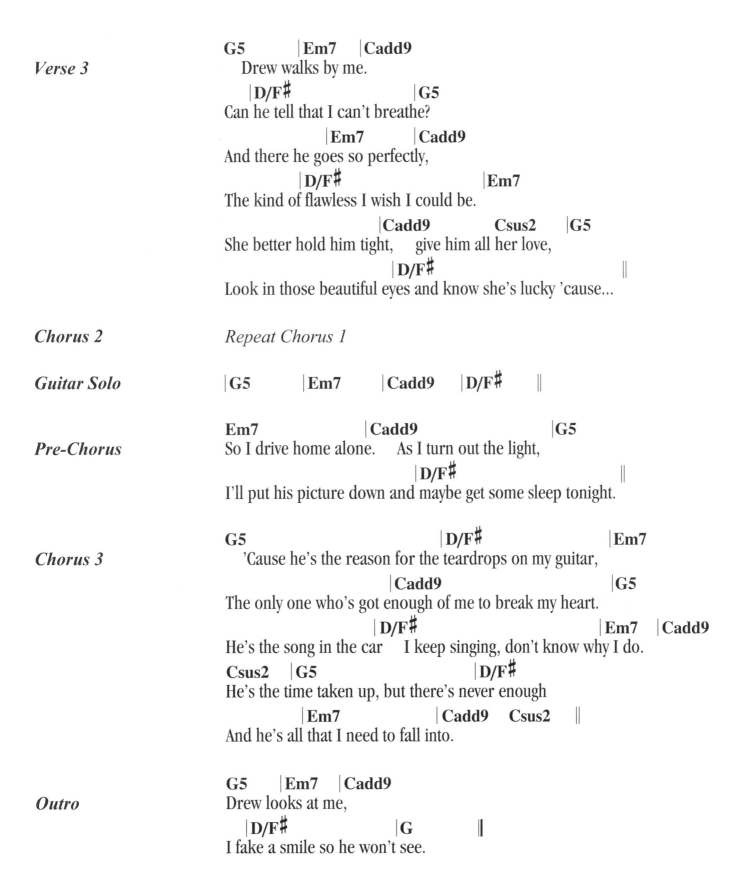

We Are Never Ever Getting Back Together

Words and Music by
Taylor Swift, Max Martin
and Shellback

Intro |Csus2   G5 |Dsus4   Em   ‖

Csus2   **G5**
Verse 1   I remember when we broke up the first time,

Dsus4   **Em**
Saying, "This is it, I've had enough," 'cause like,

 |**Csus2**   **G5**
We hadn't seen each other in a month

   |**Dsus4**   **Em**   ‖
When you said you needed space. *What?*

Csus2   **G5**
Verse 2   Then you come around again and say,

 |**Dsus4**   **Em**
"Baby, I miss you and I swear I'm gonna change; trust me."

 |**Csus2**   **G5**
Remember how that lasted for a day?

 |**Dsus4**   **Em**   ‖
I say, "I hate you," we break up; you call me: "I love you."

Pre-Chorus 1

Csus2 G5
Ooh, ooh, ooh, ooh,

|Dsus4   Em
We called it off again last night.

|Csus2 G5
But ooh, ooh, ooh, ooh,

Dsus4   Em
This time I'm telling you, I'm telling you:

Chorus 1

Csus2 G5 |Dsus4   Em   Dsus4 |
We are never ever ever ____ getting back together.

Csus2 G5 |Dsus4   Em   Dsus4 |
We are never ever ever ____ getting back together.

Csus2   G5 |Dsus4   Em Dsus4
You go talk to your friends, talk to my friends, talk to me,

|Csus2 G5 |Dsus4 |Csus2   G5
But we are never ever ever ever ____ getting back together.

|Dsus4   Em
Like,   ever.

Verse 3

‖Csus2   G5
I'm really gonna miss you picking fights

|Dsus4   Em
And me falling for it, screaming that I'm right.

|Csus2   G5
And you would hide away and find your peace of mind

|Dsus4   Em   ‖
With some *indie record that's much cooler than mine.*

Pre-Chorus 2

Csus2 G5
Ooh, ooh, ooh, ooh,

　　|Dsus4　　　　　Em |
You called me up again tonight

　　|Csus2 G5　　　　　　　|
But ooh, ooh, ooh, ooh,

Dsus4　　　　Em　　　　　　　　‖
This time I'm telling you, I'm telling you:

Chorus 2

Csus2 G5　　　　|Dsus4　　Em　Dsus4 |
We are never ever ever ___ getting back together.

Csus2 G5　　　　|Dsus4　　Em　Dsus4 |
We are never ever ever ___ getting back together.

Csus2　　　　　G5　　　　　　|Dsus4　　　　Em　Dsus4
You go talk to your friends, talk to my friends, talk to me,

　　|Csus2 G5　　　　　|Dsus4　　　　　　　　‖
But we are never ever ever ever ___ getting back to-…

Interlude

Csus2 G5　　　　　　　　|
Ooh,　　ooh, ooh, ooh.

Dsus4 Em　　　　Dsus4　|
Ooh,　　ooh, ooh,　ooh.

Csus2 G5　　　　　　　　|
Ooh,　　ooh, ooh, ooh,

Dsus4　　　　　Em　Dsus4 ‖
　Oh, oh, oh.

Verse 4

Csus2   G5 |Dsus4 Em
I used to think that we were forever, ever,

    |Csus2 G5 |Dsus4   Em |Csus2
And I used to say, "Never say never."

       G5
So he calls me up and he's like,

     |Dsus4   Em
"I still love you," and I'm like,

       |Csus2   G5
"I just… I mean this is exhausting, you know, like,

         |Dsus4 N.C.   ‖
We are never getting back together. Like, ever." No!

Chorus 3

Csus2 G5 |Dsus4 Em Dsus4|
We are never ever ever ____ getting back together.

Csus2 G5 |Dsus4 Em Dsus4|
We are never ever ever ____ getting back together.

Csus2   G5 |Dsus4   Em Dsus4
You go talk to your friends, talk to my friends, talk to me,

 |Csus2 G5 |Dsus4 Em Dsus4 ‖
But we are never ever ever ever ____ getting back to-…

Outro

Csus2 G5 |Dsus4 Em Dsus4 |
We, ooh, ooh, ooh, ooh, getting back to - gether.

Csus2 G5 |Dsus4 Em Dsus4 |
We, ooh, ooh, ooh, ooh, getting back to - gether.

Csus2   G5 |Dsus4   Em Dsus4
You go talk to your friends, talk to my friends, talk to me,

 |Csus2 G5 |Dsus4   N.C. | ‖
But we are never ever ever ever ____ getting back together.

You Belong with Me

Words and Music by
Taylor Swift and Liz Rose

Tune down 1/2 step:
(low to high) Eb - Ab - Db - Gb - Bb - Eb

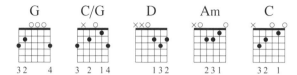

Intro |G   C/G| |G   C/G| ||

Verse 1

G | |D
You're on the phone with your girlfriend, she's upset.
                              | |Am
She's going off about something that you said
                              | |C | N.C. |
'Cause she doesn't get your humor like I do.
G | |D
I'm in the room, it's a typical Tuesday night.
                                    | |Am
I'm listening to the kind of music she doesn't like,
                              | |C |
And she'll never know your story like I do.

Pre-Chorus 1

|| **Am** | **C** |
But she wears short skirts, I wear T-shirts.

G | **D** |
She's cheer captain and I'm on the bleachers

Am | **C**
Dreaming 'bout the day when you wake up and find

                | **Dsus4** |
That what you're   looking for has been here the whole time.

Chorus 1

|| **G** | |
If you could see that I'm the one who understands you,

D |
Been here all along.

           | **Am** | | **C** |
So why can't you see, ee, ___ you belong with me, ee? ___

           | **G**   **C/G** | ||
You belong with me.

Verse 2

G | | **D**
Walk in the streets with you and your worn out jeans,

           | | **Am**
I can't help thinking this is how it ought to be.

           | | **C**
Laughing on a park bench, thinking to myself,

           |
"Hey, isn't this easy?"

   | **G** | | **D**
And you've got a smile that could light up this whole town.

           | | **Am**
I haven't seen it in a while since she brought you down.

           | | **C**
You say you're fine, I know you better than that.

           | ||
Hey, what are you doing with a girl like that?

Pre-Chorus 2

Am |C |

She wears high heels, I wear sneakers.

G |D |

She's cheer captain and I'm on the bleachers

Am |C

Dreaming 'bout the day when you wake up and find

                 |D |

That what you're   looking for has been here the whole time.

Chorus 2

                 ‖G | |

If you could see that I'm the one who understands you,

D |

Been here all along.

                 |Am | |C | |

So why can't you see, ee, ____ you belong with me, ee? ____

G | |

Standing by, waiting at your back door.

D |

All this time how could you not know?

  |Am | |C |

Ba - by, ee, ____ you belong with me, ee. ____

                 ‖

You belong with me.

Guitar Solo |G | |D | |

                  |Am | |C | ‖

                                 Oh,   I remember you

Bridge

Am   **|C**
Driving to my house in the middle of the night.
      |G   **|D**
I'm the one who makes you laugh when you know you're 'bout to cry.
|Am   **|C**
I know your fav'rite songs and you tell me 'bout your dreams.
      |G   **|D**   **|**
Think I know where you belong, think I know it's with me.

Chorus 3

         ‖G   **|**   **|**
Can't you see that I'm the one who understands you?
D   **|**
Been here all along,
            |Am   **|**   **|C**   **|**   **|**
So why can't you see, ee, ____ you belong with me, ee? ____
G   **|**   **|**
Standing by, waiting at your back door.
D   **|**
All this time how could you not know?
     |Am   **|**   **|C**   **|**
Ba - by, ee, ____ you belong with me, ee. ____
                |G   **|**
You belong with me.

Outro

             |D
You belong with me.
      | **|Am**   **|**
Have you ever thought just may - be, ee, ____
            |C   **|**
You belong with me, ee? ____
                |G   **‖**
You belong with me.

STRUM & SING

The Strum & Sing series for guitar and ukulele provides an unplugged and pared-down approach to your favorite songs – just the chords and the lyrics, with nothing fancy. These easy-to-play arrangements are designed for both aspiring and professional musicians.

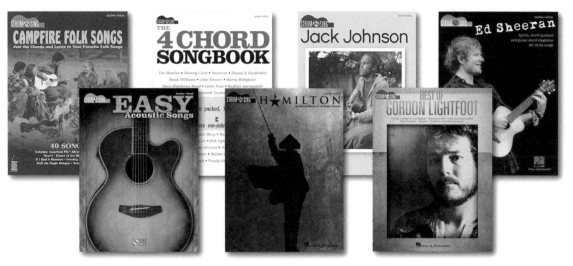

GUITAR

Acoustic Classics
00191891 ....$16.99

Adele
00159855 ....$12.99

Sara Bareilles
00102354 ....$12.99

The Beatles
00172234 ....$17.99

Blues
00159335 ....$12.99

Zac Brown Band
02501620 ....$19.99

Colbie Caillat
02501725 ....$14.99

Campfire Folk Songs
02500686 ....$15.99

Chart Hits of 2014-2015
00142554 ....$12.99

Chart Hits of 2015-2016
00156248 ....$12.99

Best of Kenny Chesney
00142457 ....$14.99

Christmas Carols
00348351 ....$14.99

Christmas Songs
00171332 ....$14.99

Kelly Clarkson
00146384 ....$14.99

Leonard Cohen
00265489 ....$16.99

Dear Evan Hansen
00295108 ....$16.99

John Denver Collection
02500632 ....$17.99

Disney
00233900 ....$17.99

Eagles
00157994 ....$14.99

Easy Acoustic Songs
00125478 ....$19.99

Billie Eilish
00363094 ....$14.99

The Five-Chord Songbook
02501718 ....$14.99

Folk Rock Favorites
02501669 ....$16.99

Folk Songs
02501482 ....$15.99

The Four-Chord Country Songbook
00114936 ....$16.99

The Four Chord Songbook
02501533 ....$14.99

Four Chord Songs
00249581 ....$16.99

The Greatest Showman
00278383 ....$14.99

Hamilton
00217116 ....$15.99

Jack Johnson
02500858 ....$19.99

Robert Johnson
00191890 ....$12.99

Carole King
00115243 ....$10.99

Best of Gordon Lightfoot
00139393 ....$15.99

John Mayer
02501636 ....$19.99

The Most Requested Songs
02501748 ....$19.99

Jason Mraz
02501452 ....$14.99

Tom Petty – Wildflowers & All the Rest
00362682 ....$14.99

Elvis Presley
00198890 ....$12.99

Queen
00218578 ....$12.99

Rock Around the Clock
00103625 ....$12.99

Rock Ballads
02500872 ....$12.99

Rocketman
00300469 ....$17.99

Ed Sheeran
00152016 ....$14.99

The Six-Chord Songbook
02502277 ....$17.99

Chris Stapleton
00362625 ....$19.99

Cat Stevens
00116827 ....$17.99

Taylor Swift
01191699 ....$19.99

The Three-Chord Songbook
00211634 ....$14.99

Top Christian Hits
00156331 ....$12.99

Top Hits of 2016
00194288 ....$12.99

The Who
00103667 ....$12.99

Yesterday
00301629 ....$14.99

Neil Young – Greatest Hits
00138270 ....$16.99

UKULELE

The Beatles
00233899 ....$16.99

Colbie Caillat
02501731 ....$10.99

Coffeehouse Songs
00138238 ....$14.99

John Denver
02501694 ....$17.99

The 4-Chord Ukulele Songbook
00114331 ....$16.99

Jack Johnson
02501702 ....$19.99

John Mayer
02501706 ....$10.99

The Most Requested Songs
02501453 ....$15.99

Pop Songs for Kids
00284415 ....$17.99

Sing-Along Songs
02501710 ....$17.99

HAL•LEONARD®

halleonard.com
Visit our website to see full song lists
or order from your favorite retailer.

*Prices, contents and availability
subject to change without notice.*